NTERROBANG

INTERROBANG

WHAT'S THAT?

WELL,
IT'S LIKE ME!

IT'S LIKE LIFE!

It's mystery
and madness
all in one!

It's like asking why
and saying yes
in the same breath!

It's like facing
this life
and wondering
about another!

It says soul
and body
in one sign!

WHAT'S THAT?

WELL,
IT'S LIKE ME!

IT'S LIKE LIFE!

It means
a bunch of
unanswered prayers
and unlimited shouts!

It's a secret symbol
for Christian cries!

It says
life is worship,
worship is a party,
and we are invited
to interrobang
without ceasing!

More balloons, Lord!
More balloons!

Interrobang! Bang!

BANG

BANG

To
my young wife Barbara
from
my young friends here and there
for
the young in Christ everywhere

ISBN 0 7188 1760 5

First published in Great Britain 1970

Second Impression 1972

Printed in Great Britain
by Wood Westworth & Co. Ltd., St. Helens, Lancashire.

INTERROBANG

‽

Prayers and Shouts

by

Norman C. Habel

Illustrations
by
Patrick Mason

LUTTERWORTH PRESS
London

THE POWER OF INTERROBANG

Interrobang has four rounds of ammunition for faith and worship. Four collections of open prayers and open hearts can be felt and used. Each of these groups can be used for personal power or for worship power.

ROUND ONE is aimed at faith and the struggle of young people to accept God, Christ, and the church in the same terms that we did. Typical teenage honesty makes these prayers powerful and pure.

ROUND TWO penetrates deeper. It searches for meaning in love. Here we find that deep longing to discover real people behind the many facades of young and old alike. The strongest hunger is one for the real love of a real Lord.

ROUND THREE centres on the great festivals of the church. These fresh thoughts on the meaning of Christmas, Easter, or Pentecost can be offered as prayers on worship occasions. They are "cool" collects for young Christians.

ROUND FOUR may be the most explosive round. The prayers in this collection are litanies suitable for use at various points in the liturgy. They begin with invitations to worship, include materials on confession, absolution, and the sacrament, and conclude with blessings. The structure is mine, the mood is informal, and the message is yours.

THE POINT OF INTERROBANG

The word *Interrobang* is relatively new. Interrobang is a symbol promoted by Remington Rand Corporation. This symbol is the first new punctuation mark since 1671. It expresses the incredibility of life today. We thank Remington Rand for introducing this symbol. We would like to promote it as a new symbol for prayer. It reflects the Christian who can shout "Yes!" amid his many questions and doubts. In prayer the question mark and the exclamation mark converge.

Adults are afraid of young people today. In general young people are so much more intelligent and honest than their parents. Teenagers I meet have an uncanny way of seeing through people after little or no conversation. Few adults in the church will risk facing youth. You kids expose us. You have exposed me many times, but some of you have asked me to let your feelings be known.

My task, then, is to open my senses to you young people and to feel some of your feelings. I gather your gripes, I select your screams, I taste your troubles, and I collect your conversations. Now, I offer them to you for your own use. I give you back your own tools for your work as men of Christ at large. They are your chance to be yourself in worship. With this box of words you can interrobang your own way, not ours.

Thanks to all who contributed. Thanks a million.

Norman C. Habel

THE PRAYERS OF INTERROBANG

LIVE

ROUND ONE

Computers are not toys
any longer.
Their circuits are
the arteries of industry,
the Book of Life
where all the deeds of men
are stored for eternity.
But computer minds
are still ignorant
of a human scheme
to outwit them
with:

PRANKS
OF
FAITH

ALL GLORY TO GOD

If I can't be honest with you, Lord,
I can't be honest with anyone.
You are the only person I know
who can take it,
no matter what I say.

People are offended if I'm honest.
They want to hear nice things,
sweet words of happiness,
gentle hymns to a gentle God
smiling somewhere
on a red velvet throne.

Well I'm sick of being phony
and I don't like to act
as if there's nothing wrong
with me
or my friends
or the world
or you.

Sometimes I want to scream at you
and let it out.
I have a million
unanswered prayers
stuck in my throat.

I want you to listen
when I yell at the sky,
pound my pillow,
kick the ground,
throw stones at the stars,
slam doors,
or swear at the world.

Perhaps that's not giving
all glory to God,
as others do,
with folded hands and frozen face,
but for me it means
I'm paying you
the highest respect there is.
It means I trust you with the truth—
all the truth.

I FEEL SUCH A FOOL TRYING TO BELIEVE

Lord,
I feel such a fool
talking to you,
trying to believe.
I'm not sure
if you're listening
or laughing
or sleeping,
or if you're there at all!

I may as well be
screaming at the wind.
My words just blow away,
drift away
and die.

But the silly thing about it is
that I keep thinking about you!
You slip through my doubts
like a chink of light,
like a haunting secret!

If only I could be positive
and really believe!
I don't have faith like that,
something solid and certain!

All I have is a funny feeling.
It's the kind of feeling you have
when you think you've met a certain
person before, but you can't quite visualize
the face or the time
or the place.
Yet somehow you know
this person knows you well.
And you could scream
because you can't quite open the door
and meet that person face to face.

And the more you think about it
the more you get the feeling
that this person makes a difference somehow,
that he has a secret campaign going
to upset people, like you,
to change their way of thinking
and laughing
and loving.

Sometimes he seems so close
that you could flick him
with your eyelashes
if only you could see him clearly.

And then you catch yourself
talking to him again.
And you say to yourself,
"I feel such a fool
talking to you, Lord,
trying to believe."

WE'RE ENEMIES, GOD

What's wrong with me, God?

I hurt my friends
and say rotten things about them.
I brag to them
and use them all like little steps
to make myself feel taller.
I pretend to be concerned
about the things they say,
but what I really want to do
is to enjoy their company
like friendly pets who do not bite.

If I stop and think
about the things I do
I get mad at myself
for being selfish
and stupid and thoughtless.
But tomorrow
I'll probably go out
and do the same things again
without realizing what I do.

Why can't I change?
I know what's wrong
but that doesn't solve anything.

Maybe . . . .
Yes, maybe the problem
is something much deeper.
Maybe the things I do
are just the surface sores,
sores that I can scratch
to avoid looking deeper.

Maybe there's some
deep internal bleeding
that is making me so frantic.

Maybe the real sickness
is a kind of wound inside
that comes from trying
to tear away from God
and live without him.

Maybe God is the trouble after all,
and he won't stop the pain
till I give in to him.
For he keeps giving me hell inside
till I surrender all my pride.

Well, if that is true,
I hate you, God.
I hate anyone who hurts me,
exposes me,
or makes me look weak.

I hate you
because you can see through me
and find me
no matter where I run,
because you can break my brain
like a bad dream.

Why don't you leave me alone, God?
Why do you hunt me
as if I were a wanted man?
What do you want with me?
Do you enjoy torturing me?

I'm just a man.
Am I so important?
We're enemies, God.
How can you change that?
How?

If only there were someone
who could stand between us
with a hand on my shoulder
and a hand on yours
to mediate our differences.

Or is that the role
that Jesus Christ, the Jew,
has been waiting centuries
to play for me
and you?

GOD, IT WAS UGLY

God, it was ugly,
too ugly even to pray about.
Men trapped in a mine.
Damn it, God,
how could you let it happen?
How? How?

People kept waiting for a sign,
a kind clue from you,
a hint of hope,
just a hint.

But nothing.
You gave them nothing.
Nothing but waiting,
ugly waiting.

Deep in the tunnels
the men kept waiting,
waiting for the next explosion,
for the taste of poisonous gas,
for the trickle of fresh air,
for the sound of someone tapping,
someone.

But no one came,
no one at all.
No one could hear them.
No one could find them.
No one could touch them.
No one.

And on the surface
they kept waiting
with an angry wait,
a sick wait,
a soul wait,
a damn-you, damn-me, damn-God wait.

They kept waiting for someone,
someone with an idea,
a new idea,
a life idea,
a saving idea,
a miracle.

But no one came,
no one at all.
No one could calm them.
No one could help them.
No one could heal them.

And then the limestone,
tons of gurgling dirt,
sealing the entrance of the mine
with the kiss of death!

The mine became a tomb,
a smouldering sepulchre,
a burning, exploding, poisonous hell.

Hell, God, hell.
Do you understand?

No one came.
There was no answer.
Ten thousand prayers,
but not one answer.

Shall we chalk it up
to the mystery of God?
Shall we blame it
on the folly of little men?
Shall we make chance
the whipping boy again
and shout to all the world:
"It's just one of those things!"

Well that didn't satisfy Job,
and it doesn't satisfy us.

Answer us.
For Christ's sake answer us.
Take us to the tomb of your own son.
Show us his limestone sepulchre,
and answer us.

We are waiting
for the sound of someone tapping,
tapping,
tapping our names
deep in the earth
among the dead.

We are waiting!

I FEEL ROTTEN, LORD

God, I feel rotten today,
frustrated
and furious
and rotten.

I feel like swearing
and screaming
and cursing
at everyone I see.

When I feel this way
it doesn't help to smile
or pray
or think about Jesus Christ
dying and rising
and suffering with me.

Nothing helps, God.
Do you understand?

It seems as if
I have a thick sponge
sucking at my stomach
and spitting back junk
that makes me sick
and sour
and mad.

There seems to be no point
in doing anything,
no meaning,
no fun,
nothing.

What's the use of living?
What's the use, God?

I have a friend in the army
lying on his guts somewhere
firing death bullets
at young people
he's never met.

What's the use of that, God?
What's the use?

DAMN
IT ALL

I have another friend
who tried to march for peace
but had his head split open
by someone who wanted blood.

What's the use of that, God?
What's the use?

I have another friend
who tried to help a woman
who was bleeding in the street
but he's paralysed for life
by a punk who ran him down.

What's the use of that, God?
What the hell is the use?

Evil and wrong
and blood and greed
make the world around me
as sick as I feel now!

What's the good
of trying to do good, anymore?
Nothing seems to work!
Nothing.

I pretend I'm a hero
and I try something good,
but it doesn't work
and afterwards I could vomit.
I feel so useless,
so sick,
so small.

I may as well get drunk,
or take some drugs,
or find some sex,
or something . . .
anything to escape.

Damn everything, God!
Everything.

Well,
do something, God.

Do something.

I WISH I HAD SOUL

I think that if I had soul
I could be someone
and really make it.

The trouble is
you can't talk about soul.
You have to feel it.
Sometimes I feel it in others,
like human radar
or human gravity
that doesn't let you go.
But I can't feel it
inside me.

You can feel soul
in the music some people play.
They can turn you on with sounds
and rhythms and melodies.
I wish I could do that.

I wish I could sing
with soul in my voice
and face
and hands
until everyone could feel
my soul.

I wish I had the kind of soul
that lives in people's eyes
and pulls you into orbit
with a kind of magic power
that is bold and free
and fascinating.

I wish I had a wild soul
that would let me fly
and fantasize
and celebrate
until I blew my mind.

I wish my soul
was a fathomless volcano
full of deep
and violent explosions.

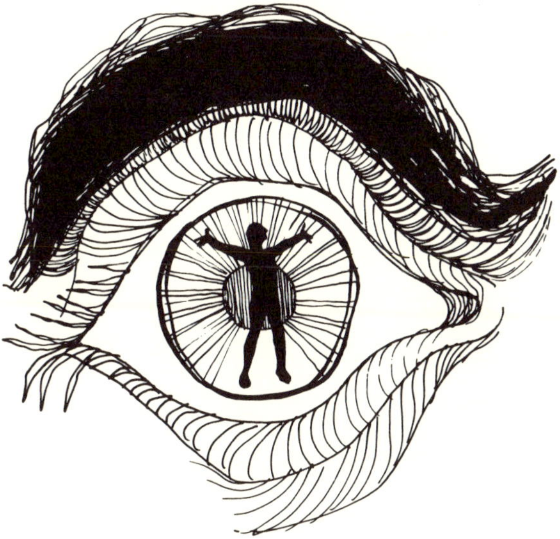

But my wishes are only wishes
and I know what I am . . .
a kid waiting for something,
and wanting . . .
wanting what others have.

If only I had . . .
just a piece of soul,
a spark,
a drop . . .
like some of the kids I know.

But I'm so ordinary.
I can't seem to understand
what gives some people soul,
or what makes them special
or exciting
or calm
or cool.

God, why didn't you give me soul
. . . or something
to make me someone?

WE'RE HUNGRY, LORD

We're hungry for something, Lord.

We have so much rich food
and cake and candy for ourselves,
but we're hungry.

Kids around the world are starving
and we don't know how to reach them.
We're hungry for them.
We want to eat with them
and listen with them.

People around us are so stiff
and tight and hard to reach.
And they make us that way.
But we're hungry for something more.

Big people tell us
to do things their way,
always their way.
They say one thing
and do something else.
We're hungry for other things.
We want to be honest
and natural
and free.

Church people tell us
to dress a certain way,
act a certain way,
and look a certain way.

But we're hungry for fun.
We want to be alive in church
and be ourselves with God.

Preachers give us God talk,
old answers and church talk.
But we're hungry for answers
that reach inside of us,
even if they hurt us.

People around us seem strong,
and sure of themselves.
But we're hungry for people
who admit what they are,
who take off their masks
and face us as real people.

People we know
keep talking about great ideas,
brilliant questions,
and the problem of God's existence.
But we're hungry for you,
not ideas or theories.
We want you to touch us,
to reach inside us
and turn us on.

There are so many people
who will counsel us to death.
But we're hungry for someone
who really knows you
and has you,
someone who can get so close to us
that we can see you there.

We have so many things,
but we're hungry for you.
Deep, deep down inside
we're hungry,
even if we appear to be silly,
lazy, or unconcerned at times.

We're hungry for your kind of power
and love and joy.

Feed us, Lord,
feed us with your rich food.

TOMORROW, BUT NOT TODAY

I'm not a shoe
tossed in a corner
or an island
lost in the sea,
I'm not an orphan
or an unwanted pet,
but I might as well be,
because I'm alone.

I'm surrounded by people,
but I'm all alone.
Some people laugh with me,
some give advice,
some ask for help
or tell me I'm neat,
but no one seems to stop
and notice who I really am.

I feel so lonely inside
that I've started spinning
a shell to cover myself
and hide
that strange something inside me
that is me.
I don't want to hide it,
but I must.
Otherwise people will see
what I'm really like.
Then they will smile and say:
"What a funny kid."

Tomorrow I'll try to leave my shell . . .
tomorrow, but not today.

I'm surrounded
by friendly people
who seem so happy.
I pretend to be happy.
and warm and comfortable, too.

I don't know what else to do
when I'm with other people.
I'm all alone then . . . .
And yet I can't talk about it
or explain why.
It's like being trapped.

I feel like a withered left hand
hiding behind someone's back.
I'm wearing a glove
to hide myself.
I need my glove,
but I hate it
because it's not really me.

Tomorrow I'll take it off
and exercise my hand . . .
tomorrow, but not today.

I'm so lonely sometimes
I could run away
and just disappear into the air.
But I want those people around me.
I want their love
and their joy in me.
Still they keep slipping past me,
slipping,
slipping away
and never really touching me.
They just see my mask
and slide slowly by.

Tomorrow, Lord, tomorrow,
I'll remove my mask
and people will have to stop
and notice me . . .
tomorrow, when I'm older and stronger
I'll remove my mask . . .
but not today,
please, not today . . .
because today I'm too alone
with so many people around me,
so many people
in this place called . . .
a church.

THIS JESUS

This Jesus.
God, he's beautiful.

I mean, he's really great.
He's not at all pretty
or "sick-beautiful"
like those pictures of him
that Christians hang on their walls.

He's not like that at all.
He's real.
He's got soul.

What he did is something else.
There's nothing like it.

You see,
when this Jesus came on the scene
God was like a stranger to people.
Oh, they thought they knew him,
but they didn't really.
Jesus knew him.
That's why he didn't fit in
with other people.
He was himself.
He didn't have to copy anyone.
He did what he had to do
and kept on doing it until
they couldn't take it any longer.

So they killed him.

He did his thing
because he was Jesus.
He wasn't trying to be someone else.
He was tough.

He cut through all the phony ideas
of the priests and leaders
and told them the truth.
And he still does.
He really knows the truth about God,
and it's wild.

"Your God is a stranger,"
he keeps saying,
"and you keep building a wall
to keep God away
because you're scared to face him,
I mean, really face him.
Well, I can bust any wall,
any evil, any box you make for God
or for yourself.

"I busted the biggest prison of all
when I jumped out of my grave
and showed the world
that God is not some stranger,
or sleeping grandfather.

"He's your Father and mine.
You kicked him out of your house,
but you can't get rid of him
and you can't kill his love,
any more than you can kill me.
Your Father and I
have started a revolution
to break open every house,
family, city, room, heart,
society, organization, planet
that locks people's lives
and blocks their view of God."

This Jesus is beautiful.

WHAT DO YOU SAY, LAZARUS?

The other day, Lord,
I saw a church bulletin board
with its witness
white on black,
archaic on gothic.

"Live each day, young man,"
the sad sign said,
"as if it were your last."

God,
I want to apologize
for that sign
and for the way we always paint you
in mournful shades of death.

Shall we start again
with black on white
and paint a sign that shouts
above the screeching horns:

"Live each day, young man,
as if it were your first."

Right, Lazarus?

Right, Lord?

Right!

ROUND TWO

I sat on the curb
where God sits
creating cities.
And I watched
the feet of men
beating rhythm
into the pavement.
I felt the earth
become one enormous
pounding city.
Then from beneath
its concrete mask
the city soul
bubbled forth in:

LONGINGS OF LOVE

A BOTTLE ON THE BEACH

I sat on the beach
like a seal
blinking in the sun,
thirsty,
dazed,
dreaming.

Beckoning across the water
I thought I saw a bottle neck,
corked
and craning for the shore
. . . or for me.

In my mind
I clasped that bottle
and plunged my finger
through the soft corroded cork
in search of mystery.

What I found
was a bottle full of prayer,
a cry for help
from a man stranded
somewhere
in the gurgling ocean.

But then it dawned on me
that maybe prayer
was meant to come in bottles,
jugs,
or cans.

My lonely friend
burning on some island beach
did not only scream at God
and leave it up to him
to take the wings of Superman
and whisk my friend to safety.

He put his prayer into my hands
and left it up to me!

Lord, it seems to me
that prayer is not a private pie
for God and me
to eat together
in a corner of the sky.

Prayer should be delivered
face to face
and man to man
where God moves in
to make his move
for help.

Anyway, Lord,
I never did like looking
at the floor
or my shoes
or the back of my eyelids
when I prayed
. . . especially in church.

Lord,
would you help me when I pray
to face my friends
and offer them what I may need
or they may need
whether it be
a bottle of prayer
a flask of wine
a canteen of water
a glass of coke
or a decanter of dreams.

Lord,
teach us to pray.

SOME VERY SPECIAL PEOPLE

I want to thank you, Lord,
for some special people that I love,
special people who love me
just because I'm me,
people who believe
that I'm important, as I am,
people who can stand me
even when I'm sour and disgusting,
people who listen
when I spit out my feelings,
people who wait
when I cannot find the words,
people who shake me
when my spirit falls asleep.

For all those very special people
I want to shout
and shout and shout with thanks.

Those are the people,
one today, one tomorrow,
who look for
that part of me that's me,
who groan with me
until that part of me is free,
who will love
whatever's left of me
when the day is over.

For all those very special people
I want to sing
and sing and sing with love.

For one like that, Lord,
means more to me
than anything on earth,
and sometimes more than you.
For only through someone like that
do I believe that you are true.
And when someone like that accepts me
in my sorry little mess,
so then do you, my Lord,
so then do you.

For every special one like that
I want to cheer
and cheer and cheer with hope.

So I want to thank you, Lord,
for that special love you give
through those very special people
you have given me to know,
and for that special love you give
when you say someone like me
is also very special
and worth the price of lonely agony
in heaven or in hell.

For that very special guy you are
I want to cry
and cry and cry with praise.

I LOVED HER

Lord, I must talk with you,
but it's not easy.

I loved a girl, the other day.

I had always dreamed
that making love to a lovely girl
would be like
bouncing slowly from a diving board
and then floating slowly
through the gentle air
until my body was surrounded
by the swirling crystal waters.

But it wasn't like that at all.
Something went wrong, very wrong.

It took a long time
before we agreed to go all the way.
We said we loved each other
and wanted to show that love.

It took a long time
before we said yes.

Then suddenly it was over.
Just like that, it was over,
and we lay there
saying nothing.

I was spent
and she was almost crying.
It was no fun for her,
not really.

And now I hate myself.
It wasn't worth it
and I hate myself for it.

It didn't help us
to grow closer,
it didn't help at all.
In fact, we're further apart.
We're like strangers.

Lord, when will I be ready
for that kind of loving?

When are two people ready for loving
so that what happens
doesn't hurt either person
but binds them both together
and gives them something meaningful?
When, Lord, when?

THEY'RE DIFFERENT, LORD

Why should I have anything to do
with people like that, Lord?
They're different.

They have a different skin,
a different face,
different talk,
different customs,
different eyes.
If I look into their eyes
I never know what they're thinking.

You made them that way, Lord,
and I suppose I should accept them,
but do I have to like them?
Do I have to get close to them?

If I'm honest with myself
I'm afraid of them,
and deep down inside I'm biased
like everyone else.

In my head I know
I should love everyone,
but it doesn't work that way.

I find myself
believing the bad things
about people who are different.
I listen to my feelings
instead of my brain,
to my fears
instead of my faith.

I can't seem to trust
people who don't think and live
the way I do.

I get scared,
the way I did when I was a kid.
I used to imagine strange noises
in the dark at night
and I would run back to the house
as fast as I could.
My parents told me
there was nothing to fear,
but that made no difference.
I was scared.

I keep telling myself
I am more open-minded
than most people I know.
Surely I'm better than some people.
How can everyone be equally important
or valuable
or worthy of my concern?

But then you come along, Lord,
and claim that you died
and rose for everyone,
no matter what they are like.
Everyone is equally important
for you
and I suppose they should be for me.

But I can't see it.
Or rather I can see it,
but I can't feel it.

The minute I get close to some people
I get angry
or scared
or tight.

Give me the spirit
that makes me open
not only to accept people
but to receive them
the way I'd receive you, Lord.

I can't do it by myself,
I simply can't.

COLOUR IS GOOD, LORD

God,
some people are saying
that you are colour-blind,
that you don't care
whether a person is black
or white
or any other colour
and so we shouldn't care either.

Well I can't accept that.

People are important.
Their eyes are important,
their names are important,
their race is important,
and their colour is important.

Because white means something,
black means something,
yellow means something,
and red means something.

Colour is good, Lord.
It's full of life.
Black people are good,
white people are good,
red people are good,
and purple people are good.

There aren't many purple people
around anymore.
The people-eaters
have almost destroyed them.

Lord, there won't be many
black, brown, white, red,
or yellow people either
if we let the people-eaters
have their way
and make us all a dirty grey.

We'll all be little robots
or Xerox people,
copied from some master copy
prepared by a cold calculating computer.

I have a hunch
that Adam was black,
Eve was white,
Cain was yellow,
and you were all the colours
of the rainbow, then.

Lord, don't let me ever forget
the importance of every little difference
between me and my brother,
me and my parents,
me and my maker,
and teach me to honour them
just the way they are.

Then I'll be proud to be
the way you made me.

IT'S LIKE A DEEP THIRST

I have to do it.
I can't help it, Lord.
The pressure builds up
deep inside of me
until there is no relief.
I have to do it.

It's like a deep thirst,
the kind that reaches
far beyond the throat.
I can last just so long
and then I can't stand it anymore.
I have to do it.
At least that's how I feel.

No one talks about it much.
But most of the kids
do what I do.
Some don't admit it
and others laugh about it.
But I don't understand
why we can't find a way
to be honest and open about it.

My parents and teachers
tell us to play sports,
or read a good book,
or go out with friends,
or pray about it.

But that doesn't solve it.
When I'm alone
the faces and bodies
of people I know
flash into my mind
and I can't help
thinking about it.

It's part of me—
a good part of me, I hope.
But I get the impression
from adults I know
that I'm rather weak
or disturbed
or sick
or something
if I can't suppress
these thoughts and feelings.

When I try to fight it
I feel as if I could explode inside
and I want release
more than ever.

I enjoy other kids.
I enjoy school.
I enjoy sports.
I enjoy being alive
with adults and friends.

But all of this contact
only seems to intensify
that deep thirst
to touch my body
and love myself,
when I'm alone.

I imagine myself alone
with one of the kids I like.
I remember the eyes,
the laugh,
the smooth hair,
the cheeks,
the warm skin
and I want them
close beside me.

But something is wrong.
It eats away at me
until I feel miserable
and very very lonely.

What I want is a way
to face these feelings,
to understand myself,
to be proud of myself,
to build myself,
and to be myself
without hurting myself.

Lord,
give me someone
who is honest enough
to admit these desires,
and to help me grow
without pretending
that God or good people
have an easy answer for me.

FOR THOSE WHO FIND IT HARD TO LOVE

My Lord,
I'm sure that you must realize by now
that you are asking me to do the impossible.
At least, it's impossible for me.
I can't love other people all the time.
I have trouble loving myself sometimes.

Other people are different
or disgusting
or dull
or dirty.
And I hate dirty people.
They make me sick.
There are some people I don't even want to love,
or like,
or help,
or understand,
or go through the agony of forgiving.
They do things to annoy me.
Or they get on my nerves
and make me mad.
Others are really enemies.
Do you understand, God, my enemies?

How can I love people the way that you demand,
forgetting about my own needs, to rescue them?
It's impossible.
And yet you say that people who do not love
do not know God.
Don't I know you, God?
I want to know you.

If you can love me all the way,
if you can surrender yourself into my hands,
if you can give yourself to die for me,
yes, if you can love like that,
you must be God, I think.
But I can't seem to love,
and I can't see you.

I strive to pose a front,
a masquerade of love
and concern for others,
for the ugly and the idiot.
But I know the sham I have created
and so do you.

You show me all that Christ has done.
You say, "Look, there is love."
I see and say, "Amen."
But after that I fall.

I need another step,
I need a lift,
I need a power,
I need something more
than this image of perfect suffering,
of Christ the love of God,
hanging on my wall.

I need you, God, within me.
I need some love genes driving me,
driving me to love,
to forgive,
and to accept forgiveness
from those I cannot love.

Please, God, may others who have loved
show me that power now to love the loveless
and the dying,
to forgive the unforgivable
and the lying,
before it is too late.

Bind me to Christ
and make me over again.

Taken from *Are You Joking, Jeremiah?*
by Norman C. Habel, published by
Concordia Publishing House, St. Louis.

LOOK ME IN THE EYE

Lately, I've wondered
what it must have been like
to look you straight in the eye, Lord,
and to hear the sound of your voice.
You must have disturbed many people
and excited many women
when you looked at them
and spoke to them
in love.

There are some people
whose eyes and voice
and presence
invade me like a beam.
They can make me leap inside
as though I were a ball
bounding for the sky.
I want to leave through the ceiling,
to escape with the wind
and fly.

Perhaps I should make my ceiling
one enormous window
so that I can watch the free clouds
spinning off
in chase of new lives.

It's all right for you, Lord.
You took off through the clouds
a long time ago.

When people touch my love nerves
I want them.
I want them for myself.
I guess I would have wanted you
that way, Lord,
if I had seen you
face to face.

Is that one danger
of being Christ to others?
For how can I love
without being selfish?

How can I free others
without leaving them torn
by my blundering?
How can I be loved
without being possessed
like a bird
in someone's web?

How can love be free?
And how can I be free to love
those you have given me to love?
Love seems to have so many
different faces
and angles
and edges.

All I know, Lord, is
that love hurts.
And I hurt
because I've hurt others
with my kind of love.

Tomorrow I may meet someone else
whose eyes can penetrate my soul
and fling me hard against another ceiling
until my bouncing soul dies
slowly and
weakly.

Lord, teach me to fly,
to come alive,
to love again,
and bounce back
for the sake of those I love.

Lord, look me in the eye!

FROM THE LIPS OF A SHADOW

Sometimes, Lord,
when the ground is warm
and the damp sky is soft,
I long to go back
past the dim familiar places
to find the first seeds
of my life
and ask why.

Plunge back with me
through my faint memories . . .
gentle fingers,
hidden corners,
midnight dreams,
and sunlit scenes . . .
to those timid waters
that spawned my life.

Come walk the sand with me
and touch my fleshy dust,
bruised by pebbles.
Listen to the crackle of light,
the screech of sunburn,
the hoarse click
of flaking clay
where once a spirit hovered
and felt its shadow speak
a word from you
of me.

Was I wanted
when the lips of the shadow were moist
and its breath was mist,
when the word was born
in crystal beads of life
floating like orange tears
upon a snakeskin-thin silence,
or when showers of colour
split the tingling silence
for me
to be?

Was I free
when the lips of the light were moist
and its breathing white
through prisms of laughter
that burst into blossoms
spluttering in the sun,
filtered in dreams
and feathered in water,
a birth-whispering water,
wet for baptizing roots
and life lines
and bone lines
and sperm lines
enveloping me?

Did you love me
when the lips of the great blossom were moist
and its breath pollenized the earth
with birth pangs below the sod,
the soil,
and the soul,
or when the face of the earth
buckled with mountainous beauty
into snow lines,
skylines,
and nightlines of power
as the shimmering evening mist returned
to hide me?

Did I look like you, my Father,
when the lips of the womb of the earth
were moist
and its breath stirred blood
to kiss the clay alive once more
and mould a boy-man,
not a toy-man,
but a boy-man,
big enough to hold life
and love life,
tall enough to see a mystery
and catch a mystery,
brave enough to find a friend
and share a glass with him?

Such is life
and the water is free
for boys like me.

DID YOU EVER DOODLE?

Lord,
did you ever do something silly,
just for the fun of it?

For example,
did you ever sit
and doodle in the air
floating somewhere
before you had this heavy world
upon your hands?

Did you ever let yourself go
and take a wild ride
across the galaxies
or tie a rainbow up in knots
without a thought
of just what someone else might think
of YOU?

Do you ever take the time to pause
and laugh with all of us?

Are the platypus and kangaroo
a couple of favourite jokes
you kept for laughs?
Are the monkeys in the zoo
a kind of sacred comic strip
on how mankind was made
by YOU?

Come on, God!
Join us in a wild spree across the city
with the wind blowing
sunshine in our faces.
Let's float a thousand enormous red balloons
in every court, cathedral, and park we find.
Let's set firecrackers
under every preacher and banker in town.
Let's paint on every single street
in hot and hairy pink
that this is resurrection day
and anyone who doesn't sing for joy
is just a silly fool.

Let's loosen up the world a bit
and use the fireman's hose
to knock the hats
off all those cats
who stiffen up their backs
and think they own this town.
Let's stop the traffic for a day
and have a ticker-tape parade
for all the orphans we have made.
Let's turn the land into a fair
and throw confetti in the air
to celebrate that you have come
to join us here.

Come on, God, let's go.

If Jesus Christ means anything
it means he's one of us.
And if his resurrection
isn't just a dream for dying men
then he's the one
who has to come
and bring this globe to life again.

BUT THE LAST WORD IS LOVE

If I talk like a man
or brag like an angel
but do not stir her love
I am as hollow as a gong.

If I sense her every mood
and fathom her mystique,
the fatal charm she has for others,
if I have the power in my mind
to change her whole life,
but have no love,
I am a wasted man.

If I overwhelm her with kindness
and smother her with dreams or dollars,
or if I leave my burning body at her disposal
but do not move her with my love,
I lose everything.

My love must be patient and provocative,
not a jealous investigation
or a selfish clutching,
not a subtle mastery
or a blunt control.

This love is more than empathy,
                more than trust,
                more than expectation,
                more than sympathy.

For it simply must not end.

My intuition will grow dim with the years,
my smooth talk will become faint,
my bright ideas will fade,
but love must live on.

I will never fully understand her ways,
her moods,
her homesickness,
or her tears,
until we cry for joy
in some new creation.

When I met her I was a child,
a foolish kid
who thought that he could be a man
and keep a woman happy by his skill
and sex
and smiles.

Now my growing pains in love
suggest another day,
a powerful tomorrow
when virility is but a slave.

Living love is like looking at a mirror
and seeing yourself change
in the face and eyes
of the person whom you love,
until each one of you
reflects the image of the other . . .
and then of Christ.

Faith,
hope,
life,
and love
encircle each other with her,
but the strongest bond is love
for she is my bride.

This poem is a
reflection on the meaning of
1 Corinthians 13 and is presented in
honour of my young wife, to whom
this book is dedicated.

ROUND THREE

They say those mansions
in the sky
were kept apart
for all those many
church denominations
from the earth.
It would be hell up there,
they say,
if Christians ever knew
their neighbours' church
on earth
was also true.
But lately
through the neon night
a song is sung
and we have seen:

FLICKERS OF HOPE

ADVENT

I. Good God,
people keep telling us
to be big and tough
and independent.
You keep telling us
that giving isn't weak,
forgiving isn't foolish,
and learning how to be forgiven . . .
well, that is something else.
It's like pushing rusty doors,
clearing spider webs,
opening an old well,
or crawling over an ivy wall.
Come Christ,
squeeze through your tight tomb
and live in us,
forgive in us,
and plant in us
your own kind of courage
to open old doors inside of us.

II. Hidden God,
wherever you are
in your kind of space,
you will have to take the initiative
to break through and reach us.
For we keep throwing up
roadblocks of doubt,
smoke screens of laziness,
sound barriers of prayer,
and endless ingenious excuses.
Break through this heavy human wall
with the blast of an embryo
and with little bits of blood.
Break through and join us,
become one of us
and shock us with your son.
Yes, shock us.
We need it.

KNOCK
KNOCK

CHRISTMAS

I. Away with the manger,
the stable, the tinsel,
the pretty round halo,
the shed full of twinkles,
the virgin's blue bonnet,
and the sweet smell of shepherds,
if these are the stories
that muffle the meaning of Christmas
and take all the bite out of birth,
the crisis from Christmas,
the bleeding of babies,
and the greatness of God
in that scared little girl
called Mary.
Away with the manger
if Christ is not seen
as the real and the raw,
as the boy left in straw,
as your God at your door
on the night he was born.

II. Lord, our Lord,
with limitless power,
we can fire men around the moon
as if it were an ornament,
a yellow bauble in the sky.
We can talk of mastering the earth
with a sweep of majesty.

We can take a close-up look at the moon
and marvel at its dusty face,
but we cannot seem to love
and find you here.

Teach us, Lord, to find the love
that lingers in the ordinary,
in babies with their bottles,
in laughter at the table,
in a hand upon the shoulder,
in the eyes of a child
with a favourite toy.

It's Christmas again, Lord.
Give us a close-up look at love,
a close-up look at God,
a close-up look
at that ordinary boy
with ordinary skin
and an extraordinary way
of saying God is near,
God is love.

Orbit our earth with love, Lord,
with that special power
for those special people
you love.

Merry Christmas, Lord.
Merry Christmas.

NEW YEAR'S DAY

Jesus, boy of Bethlehem,
you were marked as a Jew,
marked for life,
marked for death,
marked like Cain,
marked in your flesh
as a man for law and order.

Marked man,
marked for us,
bind us to yourself this year,
bind us as marked men for you.

Brand us with the word BAPTIZED.
Show us the name JESUS,
engraved on our hands,
our flesh,
our souls.

Keep these marks of freedom
before our very eyes
and never let the signs of slavery
reappear within us.

May we resolve this year
to love that child,
marked for us
to keep us free.

Happy New Year, friends.
We have a baby on our hands,
again.

EPIPHANY

Men, women, watchmen,
students on the run,
stop a minute, people,
and watch a satellite,
a star, a sun,
a signal of
a greater light to come.
For we can see
the dark and evil forces
of our sick society
invading human lives
like some heavy green gas
from the plagues of long ago.
And so we call you, God,
to unveil yourself once more
and let the fire of your light,
the sun in your son,
burn through us
and shrivel that evil
into smaller and smaller fragments
until nothing is left
but the memory.
Come in, God,
and make this a hot day,
a bright day,
and a good morning.

LENT

Robbers, rapists,
prisoners, priests,
militants, maniacs,
criminals, Christians,
listen to this man.

Today you can have it all:
freedom for life,
paradise today.

There he hangs,
king of the criminals,
lord of the laughing mob,
master of the militants,
protector of the prostitutes,
ruler of the dope rings,
director of the dropouts.

There he is, your man.
They put him in your camp,
he lived in your camp,
and he died for your camp
to take from your camp
all who wanted to go with him.

Do you want him?

There he dies,
a traitor and a fool
on his wild way to God
and willing to take along
any who can take his dying words:
"Today you can have it all.
Today you can join me there.
It's paradise today, men."

Do we want him?

Yes, indeed.
For today we confess, Lord,
that we are not ashamed
to identify that man
as the very man of God
who has given life to us,
unlimited life
today.

PALM SUNDAY

We feel for you today, Lord,
as you ride your drowsy donkey
through the crowded streets
of gaudy old Jerusalem,
alive with palms.

You suffered a hero's welcome
and learned the pain
of a hero's heart
torn by the thought of tomorrow,
when the shouting would be over.

You heard the dreams of the crowd,
a sacrifice for the crowd,
a sop to the fools,
a king for a day.

You had your ticker-tape parade
and rode forth in majesty
to receive the keys of the city,
the keys of death.

In the face of this, Lord,
can you explain
why we keep striving
to be heroes?

Let us join you
under the palms,
tonight.

GOOD FRIDAY

God.
Forsaker.
Father.

There is no more vicious word
in all the world
than the word *forsaken.*

There is no more cruel scene
in all the world
than the Lord forsaken.

There is no more pathetic figure
in all the world
than this man forsaken.

Forsaken.
Forsaken by the beautiful.

Forsaken.
Forsaken by the merciful.

Forsaken.
Forsaken by his friends.

Forsaken.
Forsaken by his God.

Forsaken.
Forsaken by the children.

Forsaken.
Forsaken by the forsaken.

EASTER

EASTER

Universe
and every universe beyond,
spin and blaze,
whirl and dance,
leap and laugh
as never before.
It's happened.
It's new.
It's here.
The liberation.
The victory.
The new creation.
Christ has smashed death.
He has liberated the world.
He has freed the universe.
You and I and everything
are free again,
new again,
alive again.
Let's have a festival
and follow him across the skies,
through the flames of heaven
and back down every alley of our town.
There, let's have him come
to liberate our city,
clean up the mess
and start all over again.
You conquered.
Keep on fighting through us.
You arose.
Keep on rising in us.
You celebrated.
Keep on celebrating with us.
You happen.
You are new.
You are here.

ASCENSION

Jesus, our Lord,
you rescued the universe for us,
you gave us the world,
you gave us our lives,
you gave us a future with you.

And yet
we often shuffle through life,
shuffle through work,
shuffle through worship
with our eyes fixed on the ground.
Lift our eyes, Lord,
to see you ahead of us.
Lift our hearts, Lord,
to find you among us.
Lift our feet, Lord,
to follow where you went.
Show us where the action is,
where your news is happening,
where you are going now,
and send us in that direction.
Send us, Lord.
Really send us.

PENTECOST

Lord of the winds
and fires of earth,
before we turn cold and hard
and blunt and brittle with apathy,
agitate our spirits.
Feed us with the flames
of love and laughter
that burn for us in others.
Surprise them again.
Surprise us again.
Surprise the earth again
by rising
and rising
and rising
within our bodies,
within our senses,
within our faith.
We ask because we can,
thanks to you,
Spirit-God-Man.

TRINITY

1. A few men said
that God was dead
and some men started weeping.
A number hoped
that God was doped
and started celebrating.
But many fear
the day is near
when God will be forgotten.
And so it's time again, God,
great and good and one God,
to show yourself again.
Expose yourself in Jesus Christ,
and show yourself
in the heaven above,
in the earth below,
and deep in us.
Show yourself
in the Word of God,
in your sons we meet,
and deep in us.
Show yourself
as you have done before.
Show us enough
to strengthen our faith,
our jittery hearts,
our searching minds,
our buckling knees,
and make your promise sure.
Be God, God.
Be God.

TRINITY

II. Lord of the oceans
above and below the earth,
send a drop of water onto my tongue.
Make it a big drop.
And drop it big.
Let it smother me with freshness
and make me cool,
so cool,
so very cool.
Ease the pains
that burn inside me.
Dip me deep,
dip me again,
dip me, dry with ashes,
into the pool of life.
Let me hear again
the words that gave me birth:
In the name of the Father,
forgiven.
In the name of the Son,
forgiven.
In the name of the Spirit,
forgiven.
And down, down,
down with the devil.
Make me fresh,
fresher than the day I was born.
Make me cool,
so cool,
so very cool for you.

ROUND FOUR

We are a race of spectators
watching a race
for happiness unlimited.
We watch
and wait
and want
and worship the race.
One day some young man
will step on the track
and shout, "Stop!"
Then over his broken body
we will speak to each other again,
find each other,
love each other,
and worship afresh
with:

LITANIES OF LIFE

(Please note that throughout this section L. *means* Leader *and* R. *means* Response. Celebrant *or* Officiant *may be used to replace* Leader *where desirable.* People, Congregation, *or* Worshippers *may replace* Response. *These litanies can be expanded to incorporate the current concerns of local groups.)*

INVITATIONS TO WORSHIP

L. Now is the time to live,
to come to the Father who creates us,
to sing to the Lord who frees us,
to dance with the Spirit who fills us.

R. Yes, now is the time.

L. Let us invite the whole world
to join us in praising God.

R. We invite the sky to thunder his word,
the earth to rumble in praise,
the sea to swirl with song.

L. Let us invite the city
to worship with us.

R. We call the traffic in the streets,
department stores,
revolving doors,
and all the people
in the yellow pages,
to stop and shout his name.

L. Let us invite our leaders
to glorify his name.

R. We summon doctor, politician, star,
president, professor, clown,
to step down
and kneel with us.

L. Let us invite the injured people
to speak with us.

R. We ask all people living alone,
the blacks and whites
who have no rights,
the unemployed and angry poor,
to tell the truth in love.

L. Let us invite those who love us
to eat and drink with us.

R. We invite our friends to know our joy,
those we love to know our Lord,
and those we long
to have beside us now,
to celebrate with us.

L. Let us extend an open invitation
to one and all
to join in one full circle of joy.

R. Join the circle, Lord,
and make our joy complete.

L. Full circle, Lord.

R. Full circle.

FEELINGS OF ANGER

L. Lord,
could you please take the time today
to listen to how we feel?

R. God, I'm angry.
Deep down inside me, I'm angry.

L. Are you listening, God?

R. I'm angry because people ignore me
and laugh at me.
They use me like a mat
and treat me like a kid.

L. Are you there, Lord?

R. I get angry when I have no fun,
when I cannot have my way,
when I can't get out,
when I'm blamed for something
that I did or didn't do.

L. Is that so strange, God?

R. I get mad at my teacher,
my school,
my body,
my dreams,
and my whole world.

L. Do you get the point, God?

R. I get mad at myself when I lose,
or get tricked,
or make a fool of myself.
And I get mad at myself
for getting mad.

L. Isn't that normal, God?

R. And I get mad at you, God,
because I cannot understand you,
or see you,
or have it out with you
when I'm really mad.

L. Does that make you mad, God?

R. I get mad at everything
that goes wrong around me
or down there inside me.

L. That's the way we are, Lord.

R. We are angry young people, Lord,
but we are your people
and we want you to accept us,
to love
and change us into men.

L. Now I come to you as Jesus Christ,
and I speak his word to you:

"I am one of you.
I died and rose as one of you.
And I know how you feel,
for I was angry too.

"I forgive your wrongs
and I will give you power
to change your lives for good.
I will help you to learn your real worth
as sons of God like me."

R. Yes, Lord. Yes.

CONFESSIONS AT THE EMPTY TOMB

L. Lord, Jesus Christ,
we come to confess our feelings.

R. We come with anxiety and sorrow,
with hope and expectation.

L. Lord, Jesus Christ,
we come to the lonely cross

R. And we see you stripped,
we see you murdered,
we see you deserted.

L. Lord, Jesus Christ,
we come to the empty tomb

R. And we see our own death,
we see our own tomb,
we see our own emptiness.

L. Lord, Jesus Christ,
when we come to the empty tomb

R. We remember how we treated
our parents,
our friends,
our neighbours,
our Lord,
and we feel sorry
for ourselves.

L. Lord, Jesus Christ,
when we come to the empty tomb

R. We see a hungry world before us,
the pain of starving children,
the guilt of war on our hands,
the terror of friends without rights,
and we know that we share in these evils.

L. Lord, Jesus Christ,
when we come to the empty tomb

R. We search inside ourselves
and we cannot escape what we are,
men caught in our selfish love,
our cold hypocrisy,
our depressions,
our loneliness,
and our frustrations.

L. Lord, Jesus Christ,
when we come to the empty tomb

R. We face you as never before,
as the one forgotten,
as the one oppressed,
as the one pushed aside,
as the one left out.

L. Lord, Jesus Christ,
we come to the empty tomb

R. To confess our guilt,
our pain,
our emptiness,
and to look for hope from you.

HEALINGS FROM THE EMPTY TOMB

L. Men of God,
why do you seek the living
among the dead?

R. Because we are afraid,
we are uncertain,
we are uncomfortable here,
and we have doubts about this man.

L. Do not be afraid,
for he has risen from the dead,
he has broken through the tomb,
he has come back to life
and he is here among us now.

Men of God,
why do you seek the living
among the dead?

R. Because we feel guilty,
we feel lonely,
and we feel lost,
for we deserted that man.

L. Do not carry your guilt any longer,
for he has taken the guilt himself,
he has buried it in his grave,
he has lifted it to his cross,
and he is here among us now.

Men of God,
why do you seek the living
among the dead?

R. Because our wounds are deep.
We have torn away from that man,
we have broken with him
and with our fellowmen.

L. Do not dwell on your wounds
for he has risen to heal you,
he has risen to forgive you,
he has risen to change you all
and bind us all together now.

Men of God,
he is not here; he is risen.

R. Yes, he is risen!

L. He is risen!

R. And he is here!

L. Alleluia!

R. Alleluia!

L. He is risen!

R. And he is here!

GLORIAS FOR ASCENSION

R. Holy, holy, holy is the Lord of hosts;
the whole earth is full of his glory.

L. I squinted through my swollen lids
(swearing at my sinuses)
to watch that battered Mount of Olives
frowning at bewildered men
there,
men blinking at a void despair
up
up
empty
as they saw the Lord
as they saw a cloud hide him from their sight
as they saw nothing.

R. Holy, holy, holy is the Lord of hosts;
the whole earth is full of his glory.

L. I saw the Lord dance
beneath the bamboo shades
where laughing children
trickled
through the smelly stalls of Hiroshima
to live the life
he gave them
before a mushroom cloud hid him from their sight
and they saw nothing.

R. Holy, holy, holy is the Lord of hosts;
the whole earth is full of his glory.

L. I saw the Lord
wander as before
across a valley deep with bones
and rancid rice paddies
where crippled friend and foe
reach out
out
out
across a clearing
fixed with muttering land mines
who bellow
burst
and fling aloft
a burial cloud of thick debris
and they see nothing.

R. Holy, holy, holy is the Lord of hosts:
the whole earth is full of his glory.

L. I saw the Lord
measure out the food and cloth
to pave the rubber-beaten streets
of bleeding cities like New York
cities broken like their skylines
broken like their sons
who see the blind smog invade
in
in
in
and hide him from their sight
until they see nothing.

R. Holy, holy, holy is the Lord of hosts;
the whole earth is full of his glory.

L. I saw the Lord
hover o'er an anxious girl
to stir a foetal life within
deep
tight
and soft
as relatives breathed in pain
until a blunt abortion
sent forth a cloud of thankful sighs
and smiles
to hide him from her sight
and she saw nothing.

R. Holy, holy, holy is the Lord of hosts;
the whole earth is full of his glory.

L. I see the Lord
no
I see his glory
quitting Sinai
quitting its cloud
to mould its flesh again
to take a sunburned face
to find the native blood of man
and come
come
come alive in him once more
until we see nothing
save Jesus only.

R. Holy, holy, holy is the Lord of hosts;
the whole earth is full of his glory.

THOUGHTS FOR OUR FATHER

L. Our Father, who art in heaven . . .

R. Father,
we'd like your undivided attention.
There are some matters we must discuss
with you today.

L. Hallowed be thy name . . .

R. It's like this.
Your name is mud in some circles.
People laugh when your name is mentioned.
For some your name is nothing but a cussword.
Restore some honour to your name, Lord.
And help us to do the same.

L. Thy kingdom come . . .

R. We have some real difficulties here, Lord.
It's so hard to see your hand at work
in the world around us.
There are so many wars and evils at large.
We want you to take over right now
and to straighten out this mess on earth.
Make this the final takeover.
And use us to do it.

L. Thy will be done, on earth as it is in heaven . . .

R. We'd like to point out, Father,
that no one seems to know the plans of heaven
and very few seem to care.
Anyway, your sons are very confused
about what your will is supposed to be on earth.
What kind of change in politics and people
will make this world free and good?
Teach us your plan, put it into operation,
and speed up your timetable.

L. Give us this day our daily bread . . .

R. Daily bread is one of our foremost needs.
Millions upon millions are starving.
The world's population is exploding.
How can we use our resources
to develop each man's pride in his own work?

As we tackle this task
give us some of the rich bread from that banquet table
prepared for men at the end of this age.
We need it now.

L. Forgive us our trespasses
as we forgive those who trespass against us . . .

R. We are rather sensitive about this, Father.
We're talking about a chain reaction of forgiving.
That's not so easy. We are proud.
We sometimes feel guilty or miserable
despite your love and acceptance.
And we find it rough trying to forgive some people.
Open our hearts to your love
and give us the power to love others now
as we will in that new age.

L. Lead us not into temptation,
but deliver us from evil . . .

R. Father, don't let us have to face
the ultimate test of obedience.
Christ did that for us.
Father, don't let us have to face
the full force of evil.
Christ did that for us.
Father, don't let us have to face death
without you beside us.
Christ did that for us.

L. For thine is the kingdom,
and the power, and the glory,
for ever and ever. Amen.

R. You are God, after all.
You have the power.
You have the plan.
You have the honour.
Take over now and rule forever.
And give us the joy of seeing it happen.
Amen.

L. Let it happen, Father.

R. And let it happen now. Amen.

SOUNDS OF THE EUCHARIST

L. In the awesome name of God,
in the victorious name of Jesus,
in the mysterious name of the Spirit

R. We acknowledge our God.

L. We summon our God

R. And we wait.

L. We are still

R. And we wait.

L. We are silent

R. And we wait.
(A brief silence)

L. We wait for the sounds of God

R. And the sounds of the sacrament,

L. The breaking of bread

R. And the gushing of wine,

L. The pain of sorrow

R. And the pulse of hope,

L. The echo of our name

R. And bread in our teeth,

L. A cup on our lips

R. And breathing at our side,

L. A voice in our face:

R. "The body of your lord,"

L. A power in our ears:

R. "The blood of your lord,"

L. As we wait for the sounds of God,

R. The sounds of the sacrament,

L. The breaking of bread

R. And the gushing of wine.
(A brief silence)

L. We hear sounds in the distance,

R. The vibration of human lives,

L. The crackle of fear

R. And the murmur of distrust,

L. The scramble for rice

R. And the tearing of garbage,

L. The shuffle of withered limbs

R. And the breaking of brittle bones,

L. The shiver of a pregnant mother

R. And the scream of a motherless child,

L. The trickle of goat's milk

R. And the sigh of rich tourists,

L. The growl of empty bodies

R. And the splash of spent blood,

L. The breaking of bread

R. And the gushing of wine.
(A brief silence)

L. We hear the snarl of a bullet

R. And the snap of a trigger,

L. The thump of lead in flesh

R. And the bite of steel on bone,

L. The sudden yell of unseen mines,

R. The constant moan of riddled skies,

L. The squeal of angry flames

R. And the cough of smoking ruins,

L. The whisper of desolation

R. And the silence of a lifeless field,

L. The breaking of bread

R. And the gushing of wine.
(A brief silence)

L. We hear the bleating of a lamb

R. And the breaking of a womb,

L. The death of a lamb

R. And the breaking of a tomb,

L. The beginning of an end

R. And a word that has healing,

L. The taste of a mystery

R. And a God who has feeling,

L. In the breaking of bread

R. And the gushing of wine.
(A brief silence)

L. And we will listen for the bursting of joy

R. And the bubble of children's faces,

L. The dancing of willows

R. And the surprise of open lives,

L. The shout of mountains

R. And the laughter of a second birth,

L. The leap of our spirit

R. And the swirl of celebration,

L. We will listen to God

R. And the celebration of God

L. In the breaking of bread

R. And the gushing of wine.

BLESSINGS FROM THE BLESSED

L. We have celebrated here together.
Let us go in peace.

R. We will not let you go until you give us power.

L. What kind of power do you want from me?

R. Give us the spirit in you that is free.
Give us the power from God that is yours.
Give us that one thing in you meant for us,
for you must be Christ to us all.

L. I offer you power to struggle with Christ
in breaking the evils on earth.
I offer you power to rise with your Lord
in freeing oppressed men on earth.
I offer you fresh bread of life
to change what is deep in your soul.
All that I have is for you.

R. Thanks for blessing us all that way.
Now may we ask one from others?

L. Why not ask from those
whom Jesus himself called blessed
in his famous beatitudes?

R. We cry to those who are poor in spirit
and the poor who walk our streets:
We will not let you go until you bless us.

L. We who are poor reply
and open our empty homes to you
where our hope can never be quenched.
We offer you ourselves and what we are,
for what we have is soul.

R. We cry to those who mourn by night
and those who weep with the dawn,
to the widows and orphans of our wars
and the victims of national evil:
We will not let you go until you bless us.

L. We who weep reply
with the story of Jesus Christ
who wept over cities like ours,
who died because of their guilt,
but who lives to weep and march again
with dignity and pride.

R. We cry to the meek and merciful
whose open hearts expose hypocrisy,
prejudice, and smooth dishonesty:
We will not let you go until you bless us.

L. We who are meek extend a human love
that Christ created in us.
We return each man to you as a neighbour,
each neighbour as a friend,
each friend as a brother,
each brother as a man,
each man as worthy of honour and love.

R. We cry to those who hunger after righteousness,
the militant and the mediators,
the pure in heart impatient for honesty,
the black and white and beautiful:
We will not let you go until you bless us.

L. We who know this kind of hunger
have a spirit that none can calm,
for Christ is liberating us in you
to stir your world with truth,
to rouse the ghetto and the gutter,
the suburbs and the schools,
before the Lord returns.

R. We cry to the peacemakers and the persecuted
who still have the strength to listen
beneath a pain and agony
that strains to kill their sensitivity:
We will not let you go until you bless us.

L. We who suffer for the Lord invite you now
to be silent for a while
and touch the quick of life,
to glimpse the mystery of God in dying men
and the pulse of Christ in human suffering.

R. Thanks for the honour of your blessing
and thanks for all that power.

L. Yes, thanks for all that power.

R. Thanks and thanks again. Amen.

*(At the close of this litany of blessing
the leader may wish to request similar
blessings from those assembled for worship.)*

DREAMS FOR CELEBRATION

L. Today the Lord steps into the air once more
to taste its colour and feel its songs. He
inhales the thoughts of children, the breath
of yesterday, the fantasies of tomorrow, and
he wonders whether his children are too old
to celebrate their dreams.

R. Let us spin him our dreams.

L. Someday soon people will celebrate life every day.

R. But we would like to do it now,
wet and wild and risen with our Lord.

L. Someday soon people will send up balloons in church

R. Turn tired old cathedrals into cafeterias

L. Paint gravestones as bright as the sun

R. Know they are beautiful, black, red, or white

L. Glimpse the face of God in their patient parents

R. Use the eyes of friends in place of mirrors

L. Bounce through the mountains on beachballs

R. Write their Christian names in the sunset

L. Become as free as that man called Jesus the Christ

R. Play football with cripples in the park

L. Sing for their supper in asylums

R. Sink their teeth into politics for peace

L. Airlift food and life to the starving

R. Have senses in their soul as sharp as radar

L. Love a man because he is a man

R. Grow flowers in their garbage can

L. Cover their cars with foam rubber

R. Turn all bombs into boomerangs

L. All bullets into blanks

R. And switchblades into tubes of finger paint

L. Slow down and wait for God

R. Run through the White House with muddy feet

L. Laugh with the falling spring leaves

R. Dance in the falling summer snow

L. Baptize their babies with love before birth

R. Celebrate Easter as angels do below

L. And hang Christmas banners from the moon.

R. Yes, someday soon people will live like that, but we plan to start right now.

L. Right now, Lord. Right now.

R. Amen, Lord, right now.